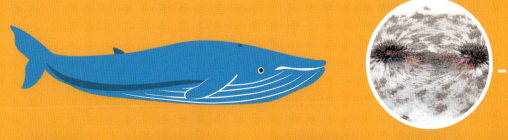

100% FORCES AND MATTER

WAYLAND
www.waylandbooks.co.uk

First published in Great Britain
in 2020 by Wayland
Copyright © Hodder and Stoughton,
2020
All rights reserved

Series editor: Elise Short
Produced by Tall Tree Ltd
Editor: Lara Murphy
Designer: Malcolm Parchment

HB ISBN: 978 1 5263 0855 9
PB ISBN: 978 1 5263 0856 6

Wayland
An imprint of Hachette Children's Group
Part of Hodder and Stoughton
Carmelite House
50 Victoria Embankment
London EC4Y 0DZ

An Hachette UK Company
www.hachette.co.uk
www.hachettechildrens.co.uk

Printed and bound in Dubai

The website addresses (URLs) included in this book were valid at the time of going to press. However, it is possible that contents or addresses may have changed since the publication of this book. No responsibility for any such changes can be accepted by either the author or the Publisher.

MIX
Paper from
responsible sources
FSC® C104740

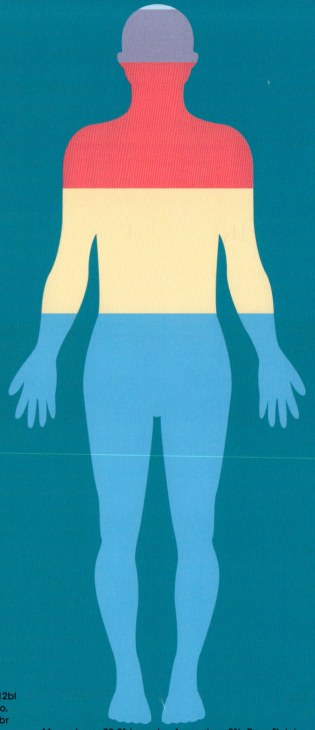

Picture Credits
25b NSF/Josh Landis, NASA: 7bl, 10bl, Shutterstock: 1tr, 12bl pippeeContributor, 1br, 14bl Taras Kushnir, 3cr, 4tl ByEmo, 3br Olexsandr Ozeruha, 4bl maxpro, 4bc Tony Strong, 4br Denis Belitsky, 5c Shutterstock, 5bl Africa Studio, 6bl StudioAz, 6cr SkyPics Studio, 7br showcake, 8bl Stellarit, 8-9 Songquan Deng, 9b McCarthy's PhotoWorks, 9r Lillac, 10tr Tony Baggett, 11tl Tyler Olson, 12tl VectorMine, 12-13 shooarts, 13b Jurik Peter, 13r Alex Staroseltsev, 14t MicroOne, 14-15 biletskiy, 15tr Istel, 15br welcomia, 16t Jillian Cain Photography, 17br Collin Quinn Lomax, 17t Avigator Fortuner, 18tl Darkdiamond67, 18-19 Sergey Ginak, 19tr Mauricio Graiki, 19b Jens Mommens, 20cl freevideophotoagency, 20cr Nordcry, 20b Nadezda Murmakova, 20-21 Irmantas Arnauskas, 21b Ryan Fletcher, 22t MicroOne, 22bl TinnaPong, 22br CKP1001, 23tr Brian Ifflander, 23cr Pixelbliss, 24l Zaid Saadallah, 24b Olesya Baron, 25t Olexsandr Ozeruha, 26bl gorillaimages, 26-27 Greg Epperson, 27r Salienko Evgenii, 28-29 Arsgera, 29t Targn Pleiades, 29bl Logvinyuk Yulila, 29br camilla$$

Every attempt has been made to clear copyright. Should there be any inadvertent omission, please apply to the publisher for rectification.

Forces and matter 4
Gravity 6
Solid matter 8
Weight 10
Magnets 12
Gases 14
Friction 16
Drag 18
Lift 20
Liquid matter 22
Buoyancy 24
Tension and elasticity 26
Pressure............................ 28
Glossary and
further information.......... 30
Index 32

Forces and matter

Forces are pushes or pulls. They affect matter, the material that makes up our world and everything in it.

Gravity
The most important force in our lives is gravity, which keeps solid objects fixed to the ground.

Gravity also stops air from floating off into space, and keeps water within the oceans, lakes and rivers.

Without gravity we would not be here.

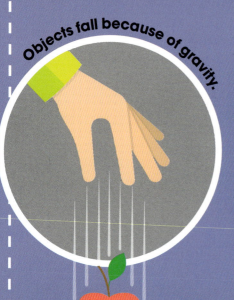

Objects fall because of gravity.

Everyday forces
Other forces affect everything humans do. For example:

Friction affects how fast you can ride a bike downhill (see pages 16–17).

Pressure inside tyres helps get you to school on time (see pages 28–29).

Buoyancy helps ships to float in the sea (see pages 24–25).

Matter

The building blocks of matter are called atoms. Atoms link together to form molecules. Molecules form the three main types of matter:

Solids

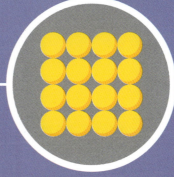

Tightly packed atoms form solid matter.

Solid matter can hold the same shape and size.

Liquids

Less tightly packed atoms form liquids.

Liquids stay the same size, but can change their shape.

Gases

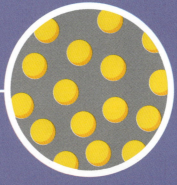

Loosely packed molecules form gases.

Gases can change their size and shape.

Magnetism makes your headphones work (see pages 12–13).

Working on matter

Together, forces and matter tell the story of how our world works. Their rules affect everything on Earth, from what makes rain fall, to why boats float and how planes fly through the sky.

Gravity

Gravity is the force that pulls us **downwards,** allowing us to stand on the ground instead of floating off like a human balloon.

Gravity and mass

All objects have their own gravity. Objects with greater mass (the amount of matter they contain) have stronger gravity. Earth is the nearest object with the greatest mass, so its gravity is what we feel most.

Gravity and distance

An object's gravity is weaker the further away it is. Earth's gravity becomes less strong as you move away from it.

Astronauts float when in orbit!

EARTH'S GRAVITY PULLS AT THE INTERNATIONAL SPACE STATION (ISS) BUT THE ISS'S MOVEMENT CANCELS OUT GRAVITY'S EFFECTS.

Zero gravity

Aboard the ISS, everything seems weightless. The crew experiences something called zero gravity.

In fact, the astronauts are affected by Earth's gravity, but the movement of the space station cancels out its force.

9.80665 metres per second

THE INCREASE IN SPEED OF A FALLING OBJECT, IF IT DID NOT MEET AIR RESISTANCE.

THE **FORCE** OF GRAVITY IS MEASURED USING UNITS CALLED 'G'. THE FORCE OF EARTH'S GRAVITY IS **1 G**.

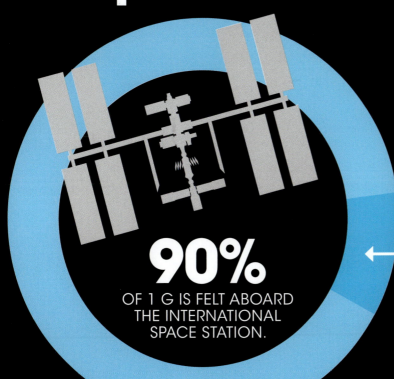

90% OF 1 G IS FELT ABOARD THE INTERNATIONAL SPACE STATION.

10% OF 1 G HAS BEEN LOST BECAUSE THE ISS IS 400 KM ABOVE EARTH'S SURFACE.

Gravity-free problems

Humans have evolved to live with Earth's gravity. In zero gravity they have problems:

- blood does not sink to their legs, which start to look all wrinkly
- their faces and heads puff up with too much blood
- their bones get weaker.

11.2 km per second is the speed a rocket has to travel to escape the pull of Earth's gravity and make it into outer space.

Blasting away at 40,000 kph!

Plant roots rely on gravity.

Gravity also plays an important part in the natural world. For example, plants have **starch grains** in their roots. These respond to gravity so that the roots always grow downwards.

Solid matter

You can identify a material that is solid by its properties – although not all solids behave in the same way. Many everyday objects, such as a desk, this book and sand, are made of solid matter.

What are solids?

Solid matter is made of **molecules** that are tightly packed together. The molecules are not equally dense in all solids, making some harder than others. The more tightly packed the molecules are, the better a solid is at keeping its shape.

Solids come in many forms, depending on what they are made from. These include metals such as **gold** and minerals such as **diamond**. But not all solids are as hard as these.

0%
THE AMOUNT A SOLID'S VOLUME CAN BE CHANGED.

100%
OF THE SPACE BETWEEN MOLECULES REMAINS CONSTANT.

Solid materials, like steel, are essential in engineering.

Diamond is a solid.

Solid qualities

Some solids can be deformed (bent or stretched), but their **volume** will not change, so they always take up the same amount of space. This makes them similar to liquids but different from gases, which usually spread out to fill space.

8

Soft and hard

Scientists use the **Mohs scale** to measure the hardness of different solids. This rates materials on a scale of one to ten, with one being softest and ten being hardest. An instrument called a **sclerometer** is used to test how easily a material can be scratched.

Talcum powder is made up of weakly connected molecules that easily fall apart.

Diamond is made of a regular pattern of carbon atoms with very strong bonds.

Mohs scale

1	Talc	
2	Gypsum	
3	Calcite	
4	Fluorite	
5	Apatite	
6	Feldspar	
7	Quartz	
8	Topaz	
9	Corundum	
10	Diamond	

INCREASING HARDNESS

Ripples on a sand dune

Solids sometimes appear to be liquid, such as when sand trickles down a slope, or blows away in the wind. But each grain of sand stays the same shape.

Heating solids

Materials have different melting and freezing points depending on their molecules. A metal pipe, for example, is solid under normal conditions and takes a lot of force to bend. Metal that has been heated until it is red-hot can be changed into a new shape more easily than cold metal. When the metal cools, it hardens again.

A blacksmith shapes red-hot metal.

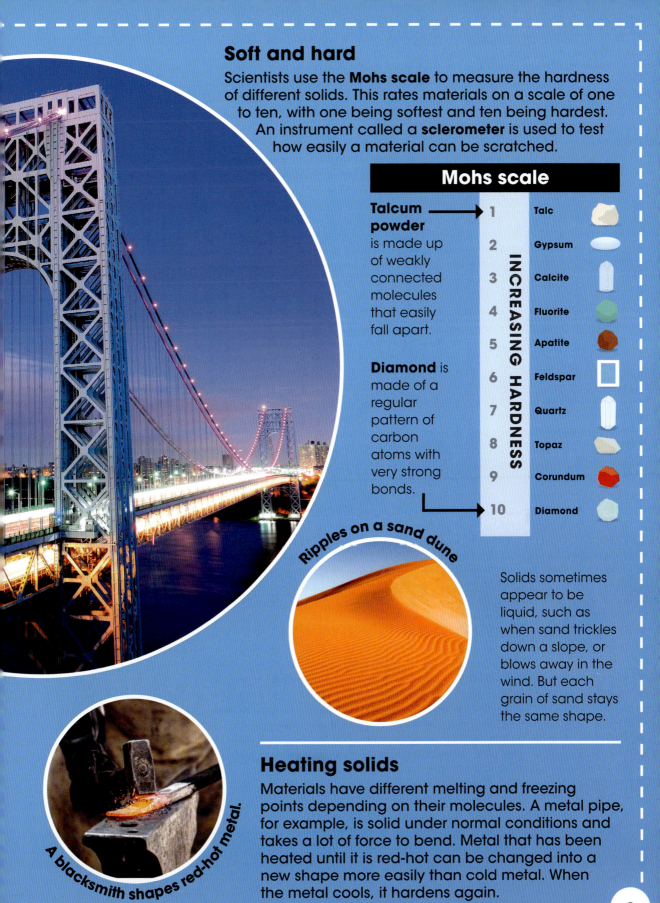

Weight

Weight is a force caused by gravity. Like all forces, it is measured in Newtons (N).

Isaac Newton

Newtons are named after Sir Isaac Newton, an English mathematician and scientist who lived from 1643–1727.

Newton developed many of the ideas of modern science, particularly those about **gravity**, **light** and the laws of **motion**.

Sir Isaac Newton

Weight or mass?

Weight and mass are different things:

Mass is how much matter something contains. It does not change, and is measured in **grams** and **kilograms**.

Weight is decided by how much force **gravity** exerts on matter.

Astronaut Eugene Cernan walks towards a Lunar Roving Vehicle.

Weight and gravity

Because weight is caused by gravity, it changes according to the strength of gravity:

On Earth
An astronaut whose mass is **72 kg** weighs about **720 N**.

On the Moon
The astronaut still has a mass of **72 kg**, but because the Moon has **83 per cent** less gravity than Earth, the astronaut's weight is now **122.4 N**.

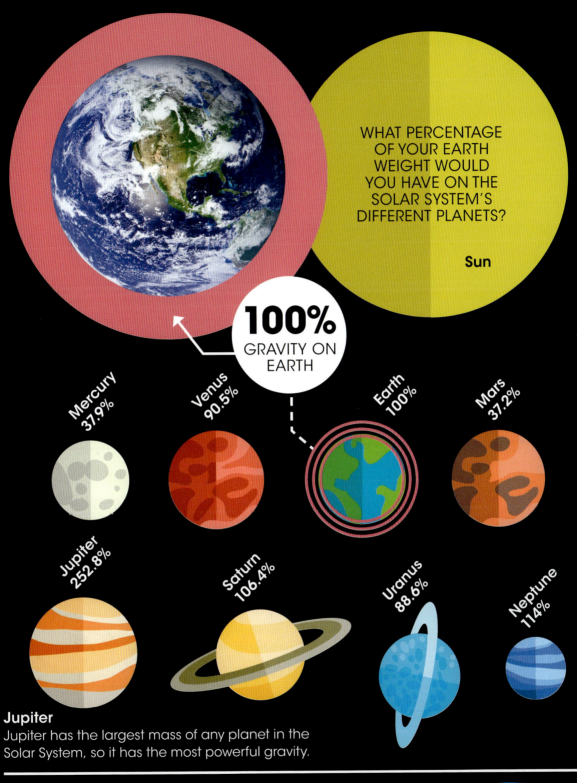

WHAT PERCENTAGE OF YOUR EARTH WEIGHT WOULD YOU HAVE ON THE SOLAR SYSTEM'S DIFFERENT PLANETS?

Sun

100% GRAVITY ON EARTH

Mercury 37.9%
Venus 90.5%
Earth 100%
Mars 37.2%
Jupiter 252.8%
Saturn 106.4%
Uranus 88.6%
Neptune 114%

Jupiter
Jupiter has the largest mass of any planet in the Solar System, so it has the most powerful gravity.

3,543,400 N

WHAT A BLUE WHALE WOULD WEIGH ON JUPITER. HERE ON EARTH IT WOULD WEIGH **1,400,000 N.**

Magnets

Magnets are objects that produce a force called magnetism. This force does not affect all matter, but magnetism particularly affects metals.

Pushes and pulls

All magnets have a **north** and **south** pole.

When the poles of two magnets are close together, they either push or pull:

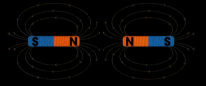

Matching poles push each other away.

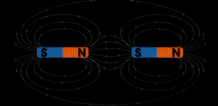

Opposite poles pull together.

Not all metals are magnetic, but all magnets are made of metal. Magnets pull magnetic materials, such as iron, towards them.

Iron filings reveal a magnetic field.

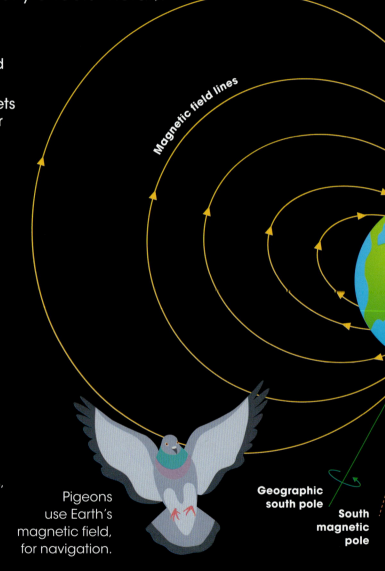

Magnetic field lines

Pigeons use Earth's magnetic field, for navigation.

Geographic south pole

South magnetic pole

Magnetic Earth

Earth itself has magnetic north and south poles. These are **slowly moving**. Each year, the Earth's north pole drifts a little towards **Siberia**, Russia. This natural process is a result of **molten metal** shifting far beneath Earth's surface.

0.0057077 kph

THE SPEED AT WHICH EARTH'S NORTH POLE IS MOVING. OVER A WHOLE YEAR, IT MOVES ABOUT **50 KM**.

North magnetic pole

Geographic north pole

Earth's magnetic force has been growing weaker over the last 100 years:

90% REMAINS

10% HAS DISAPPEARED

Reversing polarity

Several times in Earth's history, the planet's **polarity** (whether a compass points north or south) has reversed. Scientists do not know if the decrease in Earth's magnetism is the beginning of another reverse.

Compasses line up with Earth's magnetic field.

23 NUMBER OF KNOWN MAGNETARS

Magnetars are **dead stars** that have become the **strongest magnets** in the Universe. Their force is so great that they destroy nearby planets. The closest **magnetar** to Earth is about 9,000 light-years away.

Gases

Gas is one of the three main kinds of matter. It is a fluid, a kind of matter that does not have a fixed shape.

Jiggling molecules

Gases are made of **molecules** that are **spaced apart** and can move around freely. The molecules are not a fixed distance apart, so they can easily spread out.

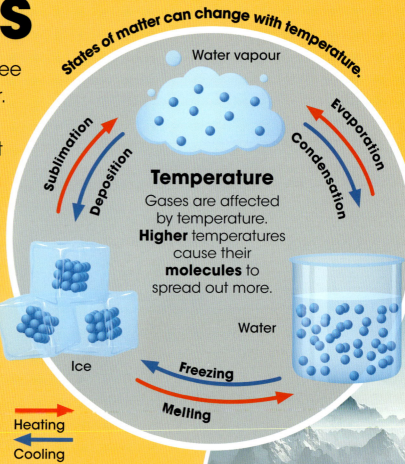

States of matter can change with temperature.

Temperature
Gases are affected by temperature. **Higher** temperatures cause their **molecules** to spread out more.

Pressure

Gases are affected by pressure (see page 28). High in the Earth's atmosphere, and even at the top of mountains, there is less air pressure. The gas molecules there are more **widely** spread out than at Earth's surface.

Air pressure is low on the highest mountains.

Temperature

All matter is affected by temperature. Higher temperatures also cause molecules to spread out more.

78% NITROGEN

The atmosphere
Earth's atmosphere contains a mixture of gases. **Plants** and **animals**, the sea and the land itself are constantly taking in and releasing these gases. Overall, the balance of gases stays the same:

Oxygen
Humans and other animals breathe in oxygen. Oxygen is needed to produce energy. This process creates waste products, such as **carbon dioxide** (CO_2), which is breathed out.

Oxygen molecule O_2

21% OXYGEN

0.03%
TINY AMOUNTS OF NEON, HELIUM, METHANE, KRYPTON AND HYDROGEN

0.93% ARGON

0.04% CARBON DIOXIDE

Carbon dioxide
Carbon dioxide is made of **one carbon** atom and **two oxygen** atoms.

Plants and trees take in carbon dioxide and use the carbon to grow, storing it in their structure and using it to make food. They release life-giving oxygen into the atmosphere.

Plants absorb carbon dioxide.

Friction

When one object rubs against another, it produces a force called friction. Friction acts in the opposite direction to the movement.

Water can reduce friction.

Friction everywhere

All moving objects experience friction.

Some objects – for example, **sandpaper** – have bumpy surfaces. These produce greater friction than smoother surfaces, such as **polished wood**.

Friction and force

When an object rubs against another with greater force, it produces greater friction: Sliding an empty cardboard box is easy. Filling the box with tins increases the **weight** pushing down on the bottom of the box, causing greater friction.

Less friction

More friction

Heat generation

Friction produces heat, which is why rubbing your hands together warms them up on a cold day.

208,000,000,000 litres

Total amount of fuel lost to friction in the world's cars. This is because a moving car has to use energy to overcome friction.

This is roughly enough fuel to drive a Smart car **4,160,000,000,000 km** (to the Moon and back over half a million times).

An average car loses a lot of **energy** to friction as different parts of the car come into contact with each other. The most energy is lost to the wheels and engine.

15% LOST TO BRAKING

35% LOST TO THE WHEELS

15% LOST TO THE GEARBOX

35% LOST TO THE ENGINE

Static friction

Objects that do not move also experience friction. A kind of friction called **static friction** exists between an object and a surface. This holds the object in place.

Static friction stops the shoe slipping

Drag

Drag is also sometimes called air resistance. It is a kind of friction that happens when a solid object moves through a fluid, such as air.

Drag slows a skydiver's fall.

Drag and size

Drag is affected by the size of the moving object. Something with a bigger surface area creates greater drag.

This is why it is a good idea to pack a parachute, rather than an umbrella, when you go skydiving.

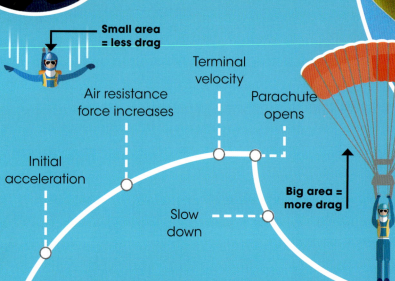

Drag and speed

The difference in speed between the moving object and the fluid affects the amount of drag. Higher speeds create more drag.

At a certain speed, so much **drag force** is pulling backwards that the object cannot go any faster. For falling objects, this speed is called **terminal velocity**.

Graph showing skydiver's velocity over time, rather than their trajectory

18

195 kph

TERMINAL VELOCITY OF A **BELLY-DOWN** SKYDIVER FALLING TO EARTH. BY TUCKING IN HIS/HER ARMS AND LEGS, TERMINAL VELOCITY CAN BE INCREASED TO **320 KPH**. IN A HEAD-DOWN POSITION, COMPETITION SKYDIVERS CAN REACH **530 KPH**.

A BELLY-DOWN SKYDIVER REACHES:

1. **50%** OF THEIR TERMINAL VELOCITY AFTER 3 SECONDS …

2. … THEN GAINS **40%** IN THE NEXT 5 SECONDS …

3. … AND ADDS **10%** MORE IN ANOTHER 7 SECONDS, UNTIL TERMINAL VELOCITY IS REACHED.

Drag and shape

The amount of drag a shape experiences is called its **drag coefficient**. Some shapes, like cubes, create more drag than others, and have a higher drag coefficient:

Sphere	Cone	Angled Cube	Cube
0.45	0.50	0.80	1.05

An object with a streamlined, low-drag shape, like a sphere, has a **low drag coefficient**.

The **streamlined** shape of a racing car gives it a low drag coefficient.

A racing car's low-drag shape is designed for speed.

Lift

Lift is a force that happens when an object and a fluid move past each other – for example, when a plane passes through air.

Helicopters use spinning rotor blades to produce lift.

Creating lift

Lift is created when a solid object forces the flow of a fluid to **change** direction. For example, a plane's wing is angled to deflect air downwards and this pushes the wing up. Lift happens when:

- A solid object moves through a **fluid** (such as a speedboat zooming across water).
- A fluid moves past a **solid** object (such as wind blowing past a kite).
- A solid object is moving **one way** and the fluid is moving the **other** (such as a plane taking off into the wind).

Speed and lift

The difference in speed between the solid object and the fluid affects the amount of lift. A bigger **speed** difference = **greater** lift.

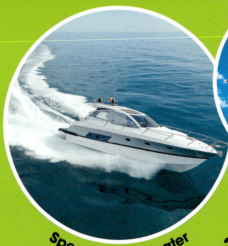

Speedboat on water

Kites flying

250–280 kph

This is the speed needed for a typical passenger jet – weighing up to **80,000 kg** – to take off.

Lighter planes need a smaller amount of lift to get off the ground because they weigh less. A Cessna 150, weighing just **700 kg**, can take off at **100 kph**.

A Cessna 150 taking off.

Adjusting lift
Pilots constantly have to adjust lift when taking off and landing. This gets the plane smoothly into the air and safely back to Earth.

Most flying accidents happen when the plane's lift is being adjusted:

58% IN DESCENT, APPROACH AND LANDING

10% HAPPEN ON THE GROUND

22% DURING TAKEOFF AND INITIAL CLIMB

10% WHILE FLYING

1 – the number of accidents per 2,400,000 plane flights.

SPECIALISED TRAINING AND **ADVANCED TECHNOLOGY** ALLOW PILOTS TO SAFELY JUDGE THE AMOUNT LIFT NEEDED.

Liquid matter

Liquids are a fluid, a kind of matter with no fixed shape. Liquids can change shape to fit their container, but they always stay the same **volume**.

The molecules in liquids are **further apart** than in solids, but not as widely spaced as in gases.

Solid   Liquid   Gas

Viscosity

Viscosity is the name given to how quickly a liquid flows.

All liquids flow, but not all at the same speed:

- **Water** flows **quickly**, because there is little friction (see page 16–17) between its molecules.
- **Thick custard** (if you make it properly) flows **slowly**, because there is a lot of friction between its molecules.

Water has low viscosity.

Water

Water is the most common liquid on Earth. It makes up about 60 per cent of an entire human body.

7% MINERALS

1% CARBOHYDRATE

16% FAT

16% PROTEIN

60% WATER

Hot water rises as steam from a geyser.

Changing state

Like other kinds of matter, liquids change their form at different temperatures. Liquids become **solid** at low temperatures and turn to **gas** at high temperatures.

Liquids freeze into solids.

Custard has high viscosity.

Liquid or solid?

Non-Newtonian liquids are odd: they are liquids that are sometimes solid.

Cornflour custard is a **non-Newtonian** liquid. If you walk across a swimming pool full of it, the custard acts like a solid and you do not sink.

Walking on custard

23

Buoyancy

Buoyancy is a force that affects objects in a fluid. It pushes upwards, against gravity.

Density

Fluids that have a **high** density produce more buoyancy, which allows objects to float.

- The water of the **Dead Sea**, Asia which contains a lot of **salt** and is very **dense**, is easy to float in – even for humans.
- Air, which is not very **dense** at all, is almost impossible to float in, unless you use lighter-than-air gases, such as helium.

Pressure

Buoyancy happens because of **pressure** (see page 28). In a fluid, there is **more** pressure lower down because of the **weight** of the fluid above.

Higher up = less pressure

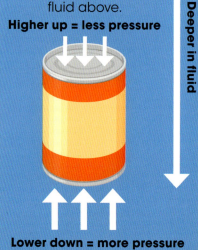

Lower down = more pressure

These people are floating in the waters of the Dead Sea.

Floating icebergs

Icebergs **float** in the sea because of buoyancy. Buoyancy increases when an object **displaces** more fluid. The iceberg has to sink down until enough water has been displaced, and the iceberg is able to float.

12.5% OF AN ICEBERG IS VISIBLE

At the **bottom** of the iceberg, the **upwards pressure** is big enough to hold it in place, with its **tip** just above the surface.

87.5% IS BELOW THE WATER

11,007 km²

SIZE OF THE LARGEST ICEBERG YET RECORDED, WHICH BROKE OFF THE **ROSS ICE SHELF** IN 2000.

NAMED **B-15**, THE ICEBERG WAS ABOUT THE SAME AREA AS OF THE ISLAND OF **HAWAII**. IT QUICKLY BROKE INTO SMALLER PIECES.

The edge of the B-15 iceberg

Tension and elasticity

Some materials have the ability to stretch beyond their normal state, and then spring back to how they were.

Tension and elasticity

Tension is a pulling force. It is the force contained in a taut rope, string or chain.

Elasticity is an object's ability to return to its original shape. Climbing ropes are designed to be elastic:
- when a climber falls, the rope **stretches**
- the rope then returns to its **original** shape, pulling the climber back upwards.

A rubber space hopper is elastic and bounces when it is jumped on.

Bouncing

Elastic materials, such as rubber bands, store **energy** when something squeezes or stretches them (a **transforming force**). When the force is removed, stored energy is transformed into moving (kinetic) energy as the material returns to its **normal shape**. Some objects use this elastic property in useful ways. Springs in mattresses and car suspension help to make things more comfortable, while elastic rubber is used to make bouncing balls.

Slack and tight

The rope above a rock climber does not have tension – unless the climber falls off and stretches it.

At first, the **slack** (looseness) in the rope means the distance between the climber and the top is **less than 100%** of the rope's length.

As the climber falls, the slack in the rope disappears. **The rope is at 100% of its normal length**.

The rope begins to stretch and the tension increases. Finally, the **force** of tension is **greater** than the force of **gravity** pulling the climber downwards. The climber stops falling.

Slack rope

Taut rope

This climbing rope has been pulled tight.

Bungee jumping

40%

MAXIMUM AMOUNT OF STRETCH IN A TYPICAL CLIMBING ROPE. THIS MEANS A CLIMBER FALLING FROM **60 M** UP WITH **40 M** OF ROPE TIED TO THEM MIGHT ONLY STOP **4 M** FROM THE GROUND, AS THE ROPE WILL HAVE 16 M OF STRETCH.

Pressure

Pressure is a force spread over a particular area. It is measured in Pascals: a **Pascal is 1 Newton** of force per **square metre**.

Air pressure

Air pressure is the weight of air molecules **pressing down on Earth**. The molecules are being pulled down by Earth's **gravity** (see page 6).

The amount of air pushing down on you decreases as you climb, so high in the atmosphere there is **less air pressure**.

Air pressure is much less on Mount Everest, Nepal.

Air pressure at the top of Mount Everest (**8,848 m** above sea level) is about:

30% OF WHAT IT IS AT SEA LEVEL.

70% HAS DISAPPEARED BECAUSE THERE IS LESS AIR PUSHING DOWN FROM ABOVE.

A pressure-powered steam train

Heat and pressure

When a fluid is heated, its molecules become more widely spread out. If it has space, the fluid **expands**.

Inside a container, the fluid still tries to **expand**. It pushes against the sides with added **force**, or **pressure**.

Steam engines and **motor vehicles** are powered by this kind of pressure.

Pressure and area

Even when the force stays the same, pressure changes according to the area it is acting on:

- When you walk across snow in normal shoes, your weight presses down on a shoe-sized area. This produces a lot of pressure, so you sink in.

- When you wear snowshoes, the same weight is spread over a wider area. There is less pressure on the snow's surface, so you can walk across it.

More pressure **Less pressure**

8,800 pascals

Amount of pressure needed to **blow your nose**.

A heartbeat produces **13,000–19,000** pascals of pressure. Between **heartbeats**, the pressure in your **circulatory system** drops to **8,000–12,000** Pascals.

Glossary

Air resistance
Also called drag, this is the force caused by a solid object moving through the air.

Air pressure
The weight of air pressing down from above. Air pressure changes with temperature and altitude.

Compass
A device that always points to the magnetic north pole.

Condensation
When a substance cools and loses energy, it condenses into a liquid.

Dense
Thick; an object or fluid with a lot of matter contained in a small volume is dense.

Deposition
The transition from a gas to a solid without becoming a liquid in between. This only happens in certain conditions.

Displace
To push out, or force to move, to a new location.

Evaporation
When a liquid reaches its boiling point and starts changing into a gas.

Evolve
To improve over a long period of time, usually into something more advanced.

Expand
To grow larger or take up more space.

Gearbox
The part of a vehicle that uses engine power to drive the wheels.

Geyser
A natural hot spring where water occasionally boils sending hot water and steam bursting out of the ground.

Mass
The amount of matter an object contains.

Pole
The end of a magnet, where its magnetic field is strongest. Magnets have north and south poles.

Protein
Made up of a sequence of amino acids. Different proteins are made out of unique sequences of amino acids, depending on their function.

Slack
Loose. When describing a rope, string or something similar, slack means the amount it can be pulled until it becomes taut.

Sublimation
The opposite of deposition. When a solid changes into a gas without becoming a liquid in between.

Submerged
When something is beneath the surface of a liquid.

Taut
Tight and unable to stretch any further.

Volume
The amount of space something (for example a solid, liquid or gas) takes up.

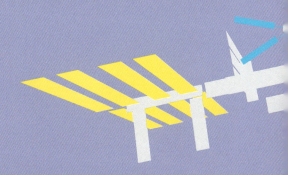

FURTHER INFORMATION

Books to read

Science in Infographics: Forces
Jon Richards and Ed Simkins (Wayland, 2017)
Part of a great series of infographics books, which make tricky subjects easy to understand – especially if you find a visual presentation of how things work helpful.

Science in a Flash! Forces
Georgia Amson-Bradshaw
(Franklin Watts, 2017)
This contains not only information about forces, starting with a flash headline then exploring further, as well as jokes and cartoons.

Superpower Science: Masters of Matter and *Fantastic Forces and Motion*
Joy Lin and Alan Brown (Wayland, 2018)
It would be great to have superpowers like a character in a Hollywood movie – but how scientifically realistic would that be? *Masters of Matter* applies scientific principles to superpowers; it also promises to make you super-smart.

Places to visit

The Science Museum
Exhibition Road
South Kensington
London SW7 2DD
The museum has plenty of displays about forces and matter, including an excellent Energy Hall where you can find out how steam powered British industry. Find out more at sciencemuseum.org.uk.

Museum of Science and Industry
Liverpool Rd
Manchester M3 4FP
Visitors can see forces in action in gas and steam engines in the Power Hall, as well as the Air and Space Hall. The museum's website is at msimanchester.org.uk

Eureka! The National Children's Museum
Discovery Road, Halifax HX1 2NE
A fantastic museum aimed completely at young visitors, where you can do your own experiments, work alongside a real-life scientist, and get tips from Science Explainers.

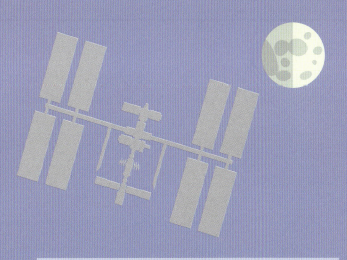

HOW TO READ BIG NUMBERS
1,000,000,000,000,000,000,000,000,000,000 = one nonillion
1,000,000,000,000,000,000,000,000,000 = one octillion
1,000,000,000,000,000,000,000,000 = one septillion
1,000,000,000,000,000,000,000 = one sextillion
1,000,000,000,000,000,000 = one quintillion
1,000,000,000,000,000 = one quadrillion
1,000,000,000,000 = one trillion
1,000,000,000 = one billion
1,000,000 = one million
1,000 = one thousand
100 = one hundred
10 = ten
1 = one

Index

air pressure 28
air resistance 7, 18–19
astronauts 6, 10
atmosphere 15
atoms 5

bikes 5
blue whale 11
bouncing 26
buoyancy 4, 24–25

carbon dioxide 15
cars 17, 19
compasses 13
condensation 14
custard 22, 23

Dead Sea 24
deposition 14
diamond 8, 9
drag 18–19
drag coefficient 19

Earth 5, 6, 7, 10, 11, 12, 13, 15, 28
elasticity 26–27
evaporation 14
Everest, Mount 28

freezing 9, 14
friction 4, 16–17

gases 5, 8, 14–15, 22, 23
gold 8

gravity 4, 6–7, 10, 28

headphones 5
helicopter 20

ice 14
icebergs 25
International Space Station 6, 7

lift 20–21
liquids 5, 8, 22–23

magnetars 13
magnetism 5, 12, 13
magnets 12–13
mass 5, 10
melting 9, 14
minerals 8
Mohs scale 9
molecules 5, 8, 14, 28
Moon 10, 17

Newton, Sir Isaac 9
non-Newtonian liquids 23

oxygen 15

parachute 18
pigeons 12
planes 20, 21
poles, magnetic 12, 13
pressure 4, 14, 24, 25, 28–29

rain 5
rocket 7
roots 7
ropes 26, 27

sand 8, 9
sclerometer 9
ships 4
skydivers 18, 19
snowshoes 29
solids 5, 8–9, 22, 23
space 4
space hoppers 26
starch grains 7
static friction 17
steam engines 29
steel 8
sublimation 14

talcum powder 9
temperature 14, 23
tension 26–27
terminal velocity 18, 19
tyres 5

viscosity 22, 23

water 4, 14, 16, 22, 23, 25
water vapour 14
weight 10–11, 24

zero gravity 6, 7

32

100%
GET THE WHOLE PICTURE

Series contents lists

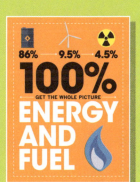

ENERGY AND FUEL
- Energy and fuel
- Energy use • Fossil-fuelled world • Electricity
- Oil • Coal • Gas
- Hydropower • Solar power • Wind power
- Geothermal energy
- Wave and tidal energy
- Nuclear power

FORCES AND MATTER
- Forces and matter
- Gravity • Solid matter
- Weight • Magnetism
- Gaseous matter
- Friction • Drag
- Lift • Liquid matter
- Buoyancy • Tension
- Pressure

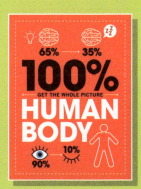

HUMAN BODY
- Human • Heart
- Blood • Kidneys
- Brain • Nerves
- Eyes • Teeth
- Stomach • Intestines
- Lungs • Bones
- Joints and muscles

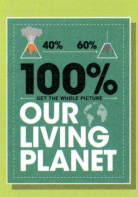

OUR LIVING PLANET
- Living planet
- The atmosphere
- Water • Oceans
- Earth's heat
- Earthquakes
- Tsunamis • Deserts
- Hurricanes, cyclones and typhoons • Forests
- Wildfires • Mountains
- Cities

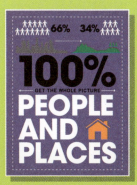

PEOPLE AND PLACES
- People and places
- Cities and countryside
- Tropical rainforests
- Temperate rainforests
- Mountains
- Lakes and rivers
- Coasts • Islands
- The Arctic • Tundra
- Deserts
- Grassland life • Space

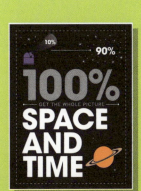

SPACE AND TIME
- Space and time
- The Big Bang
- Time begins
- The Universe
- Dark matter • Stars
- Black holes • Galaxies
- The Solar System
- The Sun • Earth
- Hours and days
- Standardizing time